The Clarence Thomas Effect: Shaping The Legal History

Alia W. Kendricks

Table of contents

DISCLAIMER

The following book is for informational purposes only. The information presented is without contract or any type of guarantee assurance. While every caution has been taken to provide accurate and current information, it is solely the reader's responsibility to check all information contained in this article before relying upon it.

Neither the author nor publisher can be held accountable for any errors or omissions. Under no circumstances will any legal responsibility or blame be held against the author or publisher for any reparation, damages, or monetary loss due to the information presented, either directly or indirectly.

Trademarks and pictures are used without permission.
Use of the trademark is not authorised by, associated
with, or sponsored by the trademark owners. All
trademarks and pictures used within this book are used
with no intent to infringe on the trademark owners and
only used for clarifying purposes.
This book is not sponsored by or affiliated with Clarence
Thomas, it is just his detailed biography from a very
reliable close source , or any Entertainment Industry or
political party , or anyone involved with them.

Introduction

In the corridors of legal history, few figures have elicited as much debate, admiration, and scrutiny as Clarence Thomas. His journey from humble beginnings to the highest court in the land has not only shaped the jurisprudential landscape but also ignited impassioned discussions on the very nature of justice, ideology, and the role of the judiciary in modern America.

"The Clarence Thomas Effect: Shaping The Legal History" endeavours to unravel the complexities and significance of this influential figure's impact. This book seeks to delve into the multifaceted layers of Justice Thomas's life, his judicial philosophy, and the seismic influence he wields within the annals of American law.

From his formative years, marked by challenges and inspirations, to his contentious confirmation hearings and his subsequent tenure on the Supreme Court, this book navigates the pivotal milestones that have defined Clarence Thomas's trajectory. It explores the legal precedents he has set, the dissenting opinions that stirred debate, and the societal reverberations of his jurisprudence.

Beyond the bench, Clarence Thomas's imprint extends, shaping conversations on race, justice, and the boundaries of judicial interpretation. This book aims to paint a comprehensive portrait of a jurist whose impact transcends the confines of the courtroom.

Join us on an illuminating journey through the life, decisions, controversies, and enduring legacy of Clarence Thomas, a man whose effect on legal history continues to reverberate and influence the very fabric of the American legal system.

CHAPTER 1: Who is Clarence Thomas

Clarence Thomas (conceived June 23, 1948) is an American legal counsellor and law specialist who fills in as a partner equity of the High Court of the US. He was designated by President George H. W. Hedge succeeded Thurgood Marshall and served beginning around 1991. After Marshall, Thomas is the second African American to serve on the High Court and has been its longest-serving part since Anthony Kennedy's retirement in 2018. He has been the Court's oldest member since 2022, when Stephen Breyer retired.

Thomas was brought into the world in Pin Point, Georgia. After his dad deserted the family, he was brought by his granddad up in a poor Gullah people group close to Savannah. Thomas initially intended to become a priest in the Catholic Church after growing up a devout Catholic, but he became dissatisfied with the church's insufficient efforts to combat racism. He abandoned his desire of turning into a pastor to go to the School of the Blessed Cross and later Yale Graduate school, where he was impacted by various moderate creators, quite like Thomas Sowell. After graduating, he was named as an associate principal legal officer in Missouri and later entered private practice there. He turned into an official colleague to U.S. Congressperson John Danforth in 1979, and was made Partner Secretary for Social equality at the U.S. Division of Training in 1981. President Ronald Reagan delegated Thomas as Executive of the Equivalent Work Opportunity Commission (EEOC) the following year.

President George H. W. Shrubbery assigned Thomas to the US Court of Allures for the Locale of Columbia Circuit in 1990. He served in that job for a long time prior to filling Marshall's seat on the High Court. Thomas' affirmation hearings were harsh and seriously battled, focusing on an allegation that he had physically bothered Anita Slope, a subordinate at the Division of Schooling and the EEOC. Slope claimed that Thomas made numerous sexual and heartfelt suggestions to her in spite of her over and over advising him to stop; Thomas and his allies claimed that Slope and her political allies had created the allegation to forestall the arrangement of a dark moderate. The Senate affirmed Thomas by a vote of 52-48, the tightest edge in a long period.

Since the passing of Antonin Scalia, Thomas has been the Court's first originalist, focusing on the first significance in deciphering the Constitution. As opposed to Scalia — who had been the main other predictable originalist — he seeks after an all the more traditionally liberal assortment of originalism. Thomas was known for his quietness during most oral contentions, however has since started posing more inquiries to guide. He is outstanding for his larger part conclusions in Uplifting news Club v. Milford Focal School (deciding the opportunity of strict discourse comparable to the Principal Alteration) and New York State Rifle and Gun Affiliation, Inc. v. Bruen (confirming the singular right to remain battle ready external the home), as well as his contradiction in Gonzales v. Raich (contending that Congress may not condemn the confidential development of clinical pot). He is generally viewed as the Court's most safe part. Thomas has acknowledged extravagant outings and gifts from Harlan Crow, a well off conservative giver, for quite a long time since something like 2004 and neglected to report them.

1.1: Early Years

Thomas was brought into the world on June 23, 1948, in his folks' wooden shack in PinPoint, Georgia. Pin Point was a little local area close to Savannah established by freedmen during the 1880s. He was M.C. Thomas, a farm worker, and Leola Williams' second child out of three. Williams had been conceived illegitimately; after her mom's passing, she was sent from Freedom Region, Georgia, to live with an auntie in PinPoint. The family were relatives of oppressed individuals and spoke Gullah as a first language. Thomas' earliest realized precursors were slaves named Sandy and Peggy, who were brought into the world in the late eighteenth 100 years and possessed by well off grower Josiah Wilson of Freedom Province. Thomas' more seasoned sister, Emma, was brought into the world in 1946, and his more youthful sibling, Myers, in 1949.

After becoming pregnant with Thomas' more established sister, Leola was ousted from her Baptist church and exited secondary school after the tenth grade; her dad requested her to wed M.C. in January 1947. Following three years of marriage, M.C. sued for separate, guaranteeing that Leola ignored the youngsters, and an appointed authority conceded the solicitation in Walk 1951. After the separation, M.C. moved to Savannah and later Pennsylvania, visiting his youngsters just a single time. Leola went to function as a servant in Savannah during the week and got back to PinPoint at the end of the week. Care of the kids was granted to Leola's auntie. At the point when her aunt's home torched in 1955, Leola took her kids to reside with her in the room she leased in an apartment with an open air latrine in

Savannah, leaving her little girl with the auntie in Pin Point. She turned to her wealthy father, Myers Anderson, for assistance after realising that she was unable to care for her two young sons on her own and that she was also unable to qualify for public assistance. He at first denied however concurred after his significant other took steps to toss him out.

Thomas and his sibling went to live with Anderson and his significant other in 1955 and experienced conveniences like indoor pipes and standard feasts interestingly. Regardless of having minimal conventional training, Anderson had constructed a fruitful business conveying coal, oil, and ice. Thomas was sent to a number of Catholic schools after he converted to Catholicism. Thomas went to the dominatingly dark St. Pius X Secondary School in Chatham Region for a long time prior to moving to St. John Vianney's Minor Theological school on the Isle of Trust, where he was the isolated live-in school's most memorable dark understudy. However he encountered initiation, he performed well scholastically. He spent numerous hours at the Carnegie Library, the main library for blacks in Savannah before libraries were integrated in 1961.

At the point when racial agitation prompted boundless fights and walks in Savannah from 1960 to 1963, Anderson utilized his abundance to rescue demonstrators and took his grandkids to gatherings advanced by the NAACP.

At the point when Thomas was a decade old, Anderson started giving his grandsons something to do during the summers, assisting him with building a house on a plot of farmland he claimed, fabricating walls, and accomplishing ranch work. According to Leola, he never showed his grandsons affection, beat them frequently, and instilled in them the importance of getting a good education. He also believed in hard work and self-reliance. Anderson instructed Thomas that "each of our freedoms as people came from God, not man", and that racial isolation was an infringement of heavenly regulation.

CHAPTER 2: Academic Pursuit

During his first year from 1967 to 1968, Thomas went to Origination Theological School, a Catholic theological college in Missouri, with the expectation to turn into a minister; nobody in Thomas' family had gone to school previously. After Martin Luther Ruler Jr's. death, he heard an understudy say, "Great. I trust the S.O.B. passes on" and "[t]hat's how they ought to treat every one of the niggers". Thomas figured the congregation didn't do what was necessary to battle bigotry and made plans to leave the ministry. He left the theological school toward the finish of the semester.

At a sister's idea, Thomas was selected at the School of the Blessed Cross, a first class Catholic school in Massachusetts, as a sophomore student from another school on a full scholastic grant. He was one of the school's most memorable dark understudies, being one of 20 selected by President John E. Creeks in 1968 in a gathering that likewise included future lawyer Ted Wells, running back Eddie Jenkins, Jr., and writer Edward P. Jones. Without monetary help from his granddad, Thomas settled his costs by functioning as a server and dishwasher in the school's eating lobby. He later reviewed, "I was 19. Holy Cross College was my only hope."

Thomas was remembered by professors at Holy Cross as a determined and diligent student. He kept to an unforgiving everyday practice of concentrating on alone and remained back during occasions to work. According to Holy Cross English professor Thomas C. Lawler, he "never talked very much in class." He was the sort of individual you truly probably won't take note". Paradoxically, he was straightforward at BSU gatherings, separating himself as a fought antagonist with Ted Wells. Future NFL running back Ed Jenkins, a BSU part, said Thomas "could change direction quickly and decrease you to scholarly rubble". Edward P. Jones, who lived opposite Thomas as a sophomore, mirrored that "there was a furious assurance I detected from him [Thomas], that he planned to get however much he could and get as far, at last, as he could".

Thomas turned into a vocal understudy lobbyist as an undergrad. He got to know about the Dark rebellion, the Dark Muslim Development, the Dark power development, helped draft the Dark Understudy Association (BSU), and showed a banner of Malcolm X in his residence room. At the point when a few dark understudies were lopsidedly rebuffed in correlation with white understudies for a similar infringement, he proposed a walkout in fight. The BSU embraced his thought, and Thomas, alongside 60 other dark understudies, left the grounds. A portion of the clerics haggled with the fighting dark understudies to reappear at the school. At the point when managers conceded reprieve to all dissidents, Thomas got back to the school, later additionally to go hostile to war walks. He took part in the violent riots that took place in Harvard Square in

April 1970. He has attributed his shift toward conservatism and subsequent disillusionment with leftist movements to his participation in protests.

Thomas decided to major in English literature because he struggled with English as a native Gullah speaker. He turned into an individual from Alpha Sigma Nu, the Jesuit honor society, and the Purple Key Society, of which he was the main dark part. Thomas became familiar with the literary works of black intellectuals like Richard Wright as a result of the college's emphasis on a liberal arts education. He additionally appreciated Malcolm X and read The Collection of memoirs of Malcolm X with the end result of wearing out the pages of his duplicate.

In his lesser year, Thomas was named a Fenwick Researcher, one of Sacred Cross' most noteworthy distinctions; in his senior year, he chose to seek after a lifelong in regulation. He graduated on June 4, 1971, with a Four year education in liberal arts, cum laude, positioned 10th in his group. Yale Law School, Harvard

Law School, and the University of Pennsylvania Law School all accepted his application. In 1971, Thomas registered at Yale Graduate school as one of 12 dark understudies. He was drawn to Yale because of its faculty members' civil rights activism and the best financial aid package. Finding it challenging to stay aware of the school's assumptions, he attempted to associate with different understudies who came from high society foundations. He signed up for the most troublesome courses and turned into an understudy of property regulation researcher Quintin Johnstone, who turned into his #1 teacher. Johnstone recalled Thomas as having "performed well overall". Both he and Hillary Clinton, a fellow student, were referred to by Dean Guido Calabresi as "both excellent students [who] had the same kind of reputation." He got a few understudy postponements from the tactical draft with the characterization 1-An after graduation, yet bombed the clinical test because of the curve of his spine.

Thomas acquired his Juris Specialist on May 20, 1974. He wanted to work as a corporate lawyer in private practice in Atlanta, Georgia, after graduation. He has said that the law offices he applied to didn't view his certification in a serious way, expecting he got it in light of governmental policy regarding minorities in society. As per Thomas, the law offices moreover "posed pointed inquiries, unsubtly recommending that they questioned I was basically as shrewd as my grades showed". In his 2007 journal, he composed: " I stripped a fifteen-penny sticker off a bundle of stogies and stuck it on the casing of my regulation degree to help myself to remember the mix-up I'd made by going to Yale. In regards to its value, I never changed my mind." Slope, Jones, and Farrington, the Savannah law office where Thomas had interned the past summer, extended to him an employment opportunity upon graduation, yet he declined.

CHAPTER 3: Early Legal Career

With no bids for employment from significant law offices, Thomas took a situation as a partner with Missouri head legal officer John Danforth, who offered him the possibility of rehearsing what he enjoyed. Thomas moved to Holy person Louis to read up for the Missouri bar, and was conceded on September 13, 1974. Even after he graduated from Yale, he had no money. He once tried to make money by selling his blood at a blood bank, but he failed. He also hoped that by working for Danforth, he would eventually get a job in private practice.

From 1974 to 1977, Thomas was an associate head legal officer of Missouri — the main African-American individual from Danforth's staff. He worked first in the workplace's crook requests division and later in the income and tax assessment division. Thomas gained a reputation as a fair but contentious prosecutor for his independent litigation. Thomas recalled his position in Missouri as "the best job I've ever had" years later, when he joined the Supreme Court.

At the point when Danforth was chosen for the U.S. In 1976, Thomas left to turn into a lawyer in Monsanto's legitimate office in Holy person Louis. He secured the position unacceptable, so left to rejoin Danforth in Washington, D.C., as an official right hand. From 1979 to 1981, he dealt with energy issues for the Senate Business Board. Thomas, who changed his get-together alliance from Majority rule to conservative while working for Danforth in Missouri, before long attracted the consideration of authorities the recently chosen Reagan Organization as the particular moderate Dark conservative supported by a compelling representative. Pendleton James, Reagan's staff chief, offered Thomas the place of collaborator secretary for social liberties at the U.S. Division of Schooling. At first hesitant, Thomas concurred after Danforth and others squeezed him to take the post.

On May 1, 1981, Thomas was appointed assistant secretary of education for the Office for Civil Rights (OCR) by President Ronald Reagan. The nomination was presented to the Senate on May 28, 1981, and Thomas was swiftly confirmed by the Senate Labor and Human Resources Committee on June 19, 1981, when he took over for Cynthia Brown, who was 32 years old at the time. Before James offered him a new position as chairman of the Equal Employment Opportunity Commission (EEOC), Thomas believed that the promotion was due to his race, just like his position in the OCR. After James counseled the President, Thomas reluctantly took up the seat with Reagan's endorsement.

Thomas led the Equivalent Business Opportunity Commission (EEOC) from 1982 to 1990. As administrator, he was entrusted with authorizing the Social liberties Demonstration of 1964 in an organization that had been commonly disdained by the two liberals and conservatives. He reported a revamping of the EEOC and updated its record-holding under an inflexible initiative that shunned racial shares. Worried by the EEOC's restricted legal power, Thomas tried to force criminal punishments for managers who rehearsed business separation, moving to move subsidising towards office specialists. Thomas opposed the Reagan Administration's plan to eliminate affirmative action policies because he thought it diverted attention from socioeconomic issues, despite his criticism of the policy.

During Thomas' residency, settlement grant adds up to casualties of separation significantly increased, while the quantity of suits recorded diminished. Civil rights advocates objected to the EEOC's lack of goals and deadlines, urging lawmakers to examine the agency's procedures; Thomas affirmed before Congress in excess of multiple times. Close to the furthest limit of his last term, the EEOC went under legislative investigation for misusing old enough separation cases.

3.1: Thomas' Rising In Legitimate Circles

In mid 1989, President George H. W. Shrub communicated interest in choosing Thomas to a government judgeship. Thomas, presently at age 41, at first dismissed the position, trusting himself unready to make a lifetime obligation to being an adjudicator. White House Insight C. Boyden Dark and White House Head of Staff John H. Sununu pushed for his designation, and Judge Laurence Silberman encouraged Thomas to acknowledge an arrangement. Expecting Thomas' selection, a liberal alliance — including the Collusion for Equity and the Public Association for Ladies (Presently) — arose to go against his bid.

Thomas was nominated by President George H. W. Bush on October 30, 1989, to take Robert Bork's place on the United States Court of Appeals for the District of Columbia Circuit. Thomas gained the support of other

African American officials, including the former transportation secretary William Coleman. He also stated that he was "struck by how easy it had become for sanctimonious whites to accuse a black man of not caring about civil rights" when he met white Democratic staffers in the United States Senate.

In February 1990, the Senate Legal executive Council suggested Thomas by a vote of 12 to 1. On Walk 6, 1990, the Senate affirmed him to the Court of Requests by a vote of 98 to 2. He created cheerful connections during his 19 months on the government court, incorporating Judge Ruth Bader Ginsburg. During his judgeship, Thomas wrote 19 conclusions.

CHAPTER 4: Nomination To Supreme Court

At the point when Justice William Brennan resigned from the High Court in July 1990, Thomas was Shrubbery's number one among the five competitors on his waitlist for the position. However, Thomas was deemed inexperienced by Bush's advisors, including Attorney General Dick Thornburgh, and he appointed David Souter of the First Circuit Court of Appeals instead. After a year, Equity Thurgood Marshall declared his retirement on June 27, 1991, and Shrubbery selected Thomas to supplant him. Shrub reported his determination on July 1, considering Thomas the "best qualified as of now". Thornburgh advised Shrubbery that supplanting Marshall with any competitor who was not seen to share Marshall's perspectives would make affirmation troublesome.

Liberal vested parties tried to challenge Thomas' designation by resembling a similar procedure utilized against Robert Bork's affirmation. The National Abortion Rights Action League and the NOW, two anti-abortion organizations, were concerned that Thomas would uphold Roe v. Wade. Conservative authorities thus underscored his own set of experiences and accumulated help from African American vested parties, including the NAACP. Other social equality associations, like the Southern Christian Authority Meeting and the Public Metropolitan Association, were persuaded not to go against Thomas, accepting that he was Bramble's last dark candidate. On July 31, 1991, the top managerial staff of the NAACP casted a ballot against supporting Thomas, reporting their resistance to his affirmation that very day.

The American Bar Affiliation (ABA) evaluated Thomas qualified for the High Court with the most reduced rating for a chosen one starting around 1955 and two of its 15 individuals rating him unfit. The Bush Administration pressed the American Bar Association (ABA) for at least the mid-level qualified rating while simultaneously discrediting it as partisan because it anticipated that the organization would rate Thomas lower than it thought he deserved. It gave its most elevated rankings to Thomas in respectability and legal personality, and a mid-grade in proficient capability.

On September 10, 1991, formal affirmation hearings started before the Senate Legal executive Board of trustees. Thomas affirmed for 25 hours, the second-longest of any High Court candidate. He was hesitant while addressing representatives' inquiries, reviewing what had befallen Robert Bork when Bork clarified his legal way of thinking during his affirmation hearings four years sooner. As a considerable lot of his previous compositions much of the time referred to normal regulation, his perspectives on the legitimate hypothesis turned into a focal point of the hearings.

Thomas claimed that natural law served as the Constitution's "philosophical background."

Ninety witnesses provided evidence in support of Thoma or against him. A movement on September 27, 1991, to give the selection an ideal proposal bombed 7-7, and the Legal executive Board casted a ballot 13-1 to send it to the full Senate without suggestion.

At the finish of the board of trustees' affirmation hearings, the Senate was discussing whether to give last endorsement to Thomas' assignment. A FBI interview with Anita Slope, a previous partner of Thomas at the EEOC, was before long spilled to the press and claims of inappropriate behaviour followed. Thus, on October 8, the last vote was delayed, and the affirmation hearings were returned. This was only the third time in the Senate's history and the first since the Judiciary Committee recommitted Justice Harlan F. Stone's nomination in 1925.

Hill, like Thomas, went to Yale Law School after growing up in Oklahoma. She told James Brudney, an individual Yale former student, about supposed lewd gestures Thomas had made, letting him know that she likewise didn't wish to affirm or disclose the charges to the Senate Legal executive Board. Hill made a request to the staff of Senator Joe Biden, who is the chair of the committee, that if she were to testify, her allegations be made in private and that Thomas not be informed of them. Biden declined Hill's request. Hill then informed Democratic staffers the day after the hearings were over that she wanted to tell the committee about her allegations.

Slope's charges were verified by Susan Hoerchner, an appointed authority in California, who likewise wished to stay mysterious. Hoerchner called Harriet Award, a main guidance to Biden, to illuminate him regarding her claims. She reviewed that Thomas told Slope in a lift at the EEOC that he would destroy her profession assuming she talked about his way of behaving. At the point when Award told Slope and Hoerchner that the FBI would be involved, they were hesitant to be explored. Slope declined to talk with the FBI, as she dreaded it would confuse her words, so all things considered organized to convey a composed assertion. The assertion portrayed how Thomas compelled her to date him, and included depictions of him talking about sexual interests including explicit movies. Slope likewise affirmed that Thomas talked about sex at work in spite of her being awkward with the subject, adding, "I detected that my distress with his conversations just encouraged him, like my response of feeling antsy and powerless was what he needed". The FBI report of its examination was not unveiled. The White House declared that the FBI had tracked down the charges "without establishment". Legislative authorities who had seen the report told the New York Times that "the agency couldn't make any inference due to the 'he said, she expressed' nature of the subject". The utilisation of the FBI was quarrelsome in the Legal executive Panel since it replies to the president, who was supporting Thomas. Biden utilised the FBI rather than the board of trustees' specialists to keep away from the presence of partisanship.

4.1: The Second Hearing

On October 11, 1991, the hearings resumed, with Thomas taking the stage first. In his initial proclamation, he rejected that he had said or successfully Slope "that might have been confused with lewd behaviour". He let the Board of trustees know that he wouldn't permit any inquiries concerning "what happens in the most cozy pieces of my confidential life or the sacredness of my room" so as not to "give the rope to my own lynching".

The board of trustees then addressed Slope for seven hours. She testified that Thomas had made sexually explicit remarks to her ten years earlier, calling it "behaviour that is unbefitting an individual who will be an individual from the Court." Her statement included reasonable nuances, and a couple congresspersons investigated her powerfully, Incline faulted Thomas for offering two genuinely threatening remarks to her: standing out his penis from that of Long Dong Silver, a dark pornography star, and saying he had found a pubic hair on his Coca-Cola can.

Thomas was brought back before the committee in the evening. He again denied the claims and was incited by Representative Orrin Portal's scrutinizing to send off a discourse that censured the procedure as a "cutting edge lynching for snooty blacks". The discourse reverberated with Southern blacks and animated Thomas' allies, with popular assessment moving in support of himself a while later. Researchers and analysts from the College of Missouri later composed that Thomas' "innovative lynching" discourse saved his selection by putting the focal point of the Senate hearings on race and bigotry and away from lewd behavior.

Slope was the main individual to openly affirm that Thomas had physically pestered her. Angela Wright, who worked under Thomas at the EEOC and had claimed that "Thomas had persistently forced her to date him and offered sexual remarks about ladies' bodies", and a proving observer she had named were not called to affirm. Their set up affidavits were placed into the legislative accounts unrebutted. Sukari Hardnett, a previous Thomas collaborator, kept in touch with the Senate board that in spite of the fact that Thomas had not bugged her, "Assuming that you were youthful, dark, female and sensibly appealing, you realized beyond any doubt you were being examined and tried out as a female."

Notwithstanding Slope and Thomas, the advisory group heard different observers. Nancy Altman, a former coworker, testified that she shared an office with Thomas at the Department of Education for two years and "heard virtually every conversation" Thomas had, but she never heard Thomas say anything sexist or offensive.

On October 13, Slope willfully took and breezed through a polygraph assessment, which her legal counsellor took as confirmation that she had been honest about the provocation claims, regardless of whether the test was not permissible as proof in court. After that, a statement from Danforth's office said that people with delusional disorders might pass a lie detector test. After the affirmation hearings finished, they turned into a focal point of isolated grant, with creators who returned to them arriving at different resolutions for one or the other Thomas or Slope.

4.2: Senate Votes

On October 15, 1991, the Senate approved Thomas's nomination as an associate justice by a vote of 52 to 48. Thomas got the votes of 41 conservatives and 11 leftists, while 46 liberals and two conservatives casted a ballot to dismiss his selection.

The 99 days during which Thomas' designation was forthcoming in the Senate was the second-longest of the 16 candidates getting a last vote beginning around 1975, second just to Bork's 108 days. The vote to affirm Thomas was the tightest edge for endorsement in over 100 years.

Thomas accepted his bonus on October 23 and took the recommended sacred and legal pledges of office, turning into the Court's 106th equity. In a ceremony originally scheduled for October 21, which was postponed due to the death of Chief Justice William Rehnquist's wife, Natalie, he was sworn in by Justice Byron White. His originally set of regulation assistants included future adjudicators Gregory Katsas and Gregory Maggs and U.S. Diplomat Christopher Landau.

CHAPTER 5: Impact On The Supreme Court Of United States

Thomas established himself as a member of the Court's conservative wing after joining. He conformed to Justice Antonin Scalia, with whom he shared an originalist way to deal with sacred translation, and favoured him in 92% of cases during his initial 13 years on the seat. Over the long run, Thomas and Scalia statue isolated, with Thomas leaning toward more grounded accentuation on the Constitution's unique comprehension and showing more prominent eagerness to overrule point of reference. His appointment signaled a decline in the liberal wing of the Supreme Court, which had only Justices John Paul Stevens and Harry Blackmun at the time.

In his initial days on the Court, Thomas embraced a striking style of legitimate statute that estranged him from Judges Blackmun and Sandra Day O'Connor. He turned into the subject of extreme media analysis for his choices, including from calculations that upheld his arrangement. Having recently experienced examination during his affirmation hearings, Thomas had confidence in creating results without respect for his public picture, a trademark which exemplified his absence of inquiries during oral contentions. His moderate methodology moved O'Connor to take liberal positions however pulled in Scalia. He framed a fellowship with Equity Byron White, with whom he shared different interests, and tracked down help from Equity David Souter.

Incorporating Scalia's narrower approach to the doctrine and original intent of the Constitution's Framers, including those espoused in the Declaration of Independence, Thomas is a proponent of original meaning. As a way to fairness, he is a backer of legal restriction to restrict legal caution. Thomas has demonstrated the greatest willingness among the Court's justices to defy precedent; as per Scalia, "he doesn't have faith in gaze decisis, period". By October 1, 2012, he had composed 475 feelings, including 171 greater part sentiments, 138 concurrences, and 166 contradicting suppositions — around 10% of the 1,772 cases the Court had chosen since he was raised. In 2016, Thomas composed almost two times however many feelings as some other equity.

Thomas has been known as the most safe individual from the High Court, however others gave Scalia that assignment while they served on the Court together. Thomas' impact, especially among moderates, was seen to have fundamentally expanded during Donald Trump's administration, and Trump selected large numbers of his previous assistants to political positions and judgeships. As the High Court turned out to be more moderate, Thomas and his lawful perspectives turned out to be more powerful on the Court. This impact expanded further by 2022, with Thomas composing an assessment growing Second Alteration freedoms and adding to the

Court's overruling of Roe v. Swim. He was additionally the most senior partner equity at that point.

CHAPTER 6: Government Power And Legal Structure- Court Precedent

Unlike the other justices at the moment, Thomas holds the opinion that the Court should not adhere to incorrect precedent. He has criticised Roe v. Wade (1973) and Gideon v. Wainwright (1963) and called for reconsideration of New York Times Co. v. Sullivan (1964). At a 2013 Federalist Society supper, Judge Diane S. Sykes found out if "gaze decisis doesn't hold a lot of power for you?" He answered, "Gracious, it sure does, however insufficient to hold me back from going to the Constitution". In 2019, The New York Times detailed that information assembled by political researcher Stephen L. Wasby of the College at Albany found that Thomas expressed "in excess of 250 agreeing or disagreeing suppositions genuinely addressing points of reference, requiring their reexamination or it be overruled to propose that they".

In the 2010 weapon guideline case McDonald v. City of Chicago, Thomas looked to revoke past points of reference and demanded that "gaze decisis is just an 'assistant' of our obligation as judges to conclude by our best lights what the Constitution implies". In Bet v. US (2019), he joined the larger part assessment, which returned to a special case for the Twofold Risk Condition, composing independently to express his situation against the Court's predominant perspective on multifaceted examination with respect to whether to follow point of reference:

In my opinion, if the Court comes across a decision that is clearly incorrect—that is, one that is certainly not a passable translation of the text — the Court ought to address the mistake, whether or not different elements support overruling the point of reference. When traditional tools of legal interpretation demonstrate that the earlier decision adopted a textually permissible interpretation of the law, federal courts may (but need not) adhere to an incorrect decision as precedent. A certifiably wrong legal choice, on the other hand, is equivalent to making regulation, and complying to it the two ignores the matchless quality of the Constitution and propagates a usurpation of the official power.

In Establishment Assessment Leading group of California v. Hyatt (2019), Thomas composed the 5-4 choice overruling Nevada v. Lobby (1979), which said states could be sued in courts of different states. As he would like to think, he noticed that gaze decisis "is definitely not an inflexible order". Thomas expressly denied the idea of dependence interests as a vocation for sticking to point of reference. In disagreement from Hyatt III, Equity Breyer asked what different choices could ultimately be overruled, and proposed Roe v. Swim may be among them. Breyer expressed that it is ideal to let points of reference be except if they are broadly viewed as wrong or become unrealistic.

6.1: Chief Power

Thomas has upheld an expansive translation of chief power and has guessed about its protected perspectives. In Hamdi v. Rumsfeld (2004), he contradicted from the larger part assessment, contending that courts ought to have had total concession to the chief choice to confirm that Yaser Esam Hamdi was an adversary warrior. In Hamdi, he stated that the president does not have sole authority to detain a citizen who was taken while serving in the armed forces. Also, that's what Thomas noticed "underlying benefits [of the Presidency] are most significant in the public safety and international concerns settings" and hence "the Organizers planned that the President have essential obligation — alongside the important power — to safeguard the public safety and to lead the country's unfamiliar relations".

Thomas was one of three judges to contradict in Hamdan v. Rumsfeld (2006), which concerned whether the president can lay out military courts to attempt confined adversary soldiers for atrocities connivance. As in Hamdi, he depended on The Federalist Papers in suggesting that the president is answerable for safeguarding public safety.

In Zivotofsky v. Kerry (2015), Thomas depended on the Articles of Confederation for his viewpoint. "The President is not confined to those powers expressly identified in [the Constitution]," he wrote, concluding that the president, not Congress, was responsible for remaining foreign affairs. As opposed to seeing as the first goal or unique comprehension, Thomas wrote for the situation that he looked for the "comprehension of leader power [that] won in America" at the hour of the establishing.

In the 10th Circuit case East Straight Safe-haven Agreement v. Trump (2018), which put a directive on the Trump organization's haven strategy, Thomas disagreed from a forswearing of stay application. The Trump administration's policy of only providing asylum to refugees arriving at a designated port of entry was found to be in violation of the Immigration and Nationality Act of 1952 by the Ninth Circuit. 10th Circuit Judge Jay Bybee's greater part assessment reasoned that disavowal of the capacity to apply for refuge paying little mind to section point is "the hollowest of freedoms that an outsider should be permitted to apply for haven whether or not she showed up through a port of passage assuming another standard makes her completely ineligible for refuge in light of unequivocally that reality." Gorsuch, Alito, Kavanaugh likewise disagreed in the choice to deny a stay to the 10th Circuit's directive.

6.2: Federalism

Thomas sees federalism as a fundamental limit on the power of the federal government. In deciphering legislative powers, he has safeguarded severe constructionism — a methodology Scalia dismissed. On September 24, 1999, Thomas conveyed the Dwight D.

Opperman Talk at Drake College Graduate school on "Why Federalism Matters", saying that it was a fundamental shield to secure "individual freedom and the confidential requesting of our lives". He likewise attested that federalism improves self-government, safeguards individual freedom by isolating political power, and really takes a look at bureaucratic power. As per regulation teacher Ann Althouse, the Court still can't seem to push toward "the more extensive, more principled variant of federalism propounded by Equity Thomas".

Nothing in the Constitution denies individuals of each Condition of the ability to endorse qualification prerequisites for the applicants who look to address them in Congress. This issue is simply not addressed in the Constitution. Also, where the Constitution is quiet, it raises no bar to activity by the States or individuals.

— Thomas, disagreeing in U.S. Service time restraints. v. Thornton (1995)

In the 1995 case U.S. Service time restraints. v. Thornton, parties moved the lawfulness of a change to the Arkansas Constitution that added additional age, citizenship, and residency prerequisites for legislative assistance. In a 5-4 choice, the High Court ruled the change unlawful, likewise confirming the past decisions of both the state's preliminary court and the Arkansas High Court; Equity Stevens composed for the larger part. Thomas — joined by Judges Rehnquist, O'Connor, and Scalia — disagreed in what is to date his lengthiest assessment. He contended that states could force service time restraints individuals from Congress, as state residents are "a definitive wellspring of the Constitution's position". That very year, Thomas agreed in US v. Lopez, which discredited the Weapon Free School Zones Demonstration of 1990 for going past the Business Statement. He thought that the Court had veered off "from the first comprehension of the Business Statement" and that the significant impacts test, "whenever taken to its coherent limit, would give Congress a 'police control' over all parts of American life".

Thomas disagreed in Gonzales v. Raich (2005), which held that the Controlled Substances Act applies to local pot, on the grounds of unique importance. His understanding of the highway business proviso contrasted from Scalia's, and they additionally held clashing convictions about the overall government assistance condition, the Indian trade statement, and the essential and legitimate condition. Scalia joined the greater part assessment, yet Thomas questioned the significance of local maryjane to highway business, composing that in the event that Congress can manage it, "it can control essentially anything — and the National Government is presently not one of restricted and specified powers".

In the US v. Comstock (2010), the High Court, in a larger part assessment by Equity Stephen Breyer, held that the Important and Legitimate Proviso permits Congress to order a regulation that approved the U.S. Division of Equity (DOJ) to confine an insane and perilous government detainee past the DOJ's unique legitimate date. Scalia joined Thomas's dissent, arguing that the clause only permits Congress to carry out a list of powers. At the point when the Court maintained the Reasonable Consideration Act in Public Alliance of Autonomous Business v. Sebelius (2012), he composed a short difference and joined the joint contradiction finding the demonstration totally unlawful.

6.3: Government Rules

Starting around 2007, Thomas was the equity generally able to practice legal audit of government resolutions however among the most drastically averse to upset state rules. As per a New York Times publication, "from 1994 to 2005 ... Justice Thomas casted a ballot to upset government regulations in 34 cases and Equity Scalia in 31, opposed and only 15 for Justice Stephen Breyer".

In Northwest Austin Civil Utility Locale No. 1 v. Holder, Thomas was the sole nonconformist, casting a ballot to toss out Segment Five of the 1965 Democratic Rights Act. Segment Five requires states with a background marked by racial elector separation — generally states from the old South — to acquire Equity Office leeway while updating political decision methods. Thomas stated that the law was no longer necessary, citing the fact that the rate of black voters in seven Section Five states was higher than the national average .Congress had reauthorized Region Five of each 2006 for 25 extra years. He stated, "the savagery, terrorising and ploy that drove Congress to pass Segment 5 and this court to maintain it does not remain anymore." He took this position again in Shelby Area v. Holder, casting a ballot with the greater part and agreeing with the thinking that struck down Segment Five.

CHAPTER 7: Individual Rights

Thomas has commonly composed feelings for insurances with the expectation of complimentary discourse. He has casted a ballot for First Correction claims in quite a while including issues including effort commitments and business discourse. A recent report by Eugene Volokh viewed Thomas as the equity second-probably going to maintain free discourse claims (attached with Souter).

He has voted down regulations managing disdain discourse, as in R.A.V. v. City of St. Paul (1992), US v. Stevens (2010), and Snyder v. Phelps (2011). On the other hand, he has been hesitant to maintain discourse considered threatening, as in Virginia v. Dark (2003).

Thomas' most memorable assessment on free discourse was the 1995 case McIntyre v. Ohio Decisions Commission, finding that the Establishing Period contained the broad utilisation of mysterious handouts and sections. Despite the fact that he concurred with the consequence of Equity John Paul Stevens' greater part assessment, he contradicted its approach and didn't go along with it. With the declaration of McIntyre, the Court additionally chose Rubin v. Coors Preparing Organization, in which Thomas composed his most memorable larger part assessment concerning free discourse. In Rubin, Thomas was joined consistently in administering a 1935 government regulation that precluded brew names from revealing liquor content. He correspondingly agreed the following year in 44 Liquormart v. Rhode Island, which struck down a state regulation that restricted the ad of costs of cocktails.

In Colorado Conservative Government Mission Council v. FEC (1996), the High Court voted down the choice of the Government Political Race Commission (FEC) to find the Colorado Conservative Bureaucratic Mission

Panel for running a political ad focusing on Congressperson Tim Wirth. Thomas joined Equity Stephen Breyer's larger part assessment for the situation, yet composed independently to call against the system laid out in the past mission finance instance of Buckley v Valeo (1976):

I accept that commitment limits encroach as straightforwardly and as truly upon opportunity of political articulation and relationship as do consumption limits. The insurances of the Primary Change don't rely on so fine a line as that between burning through cash to help an up-and-comer or gathering and giving cash to the competitor or gathering to spend for a similar reason. On a fundamental level, individuals and gatherings give cash to up-and-comers and different gatherings for the very reason that they burn through cash on the side of those competitors and gatherings: since they share social, monetary, and political convictions and look to have those convictions influence administrative arrangement.

Thomas has made public his conviction that all limits on government campaign responsibilities are unlawful and should be struck down.

In Residents Joined v. FEC (2010), Thomas joined the greater part however contradicted to some degree, contending that the Bipartisan Lobby Change Act's disclaimer and divulgence prerequisites were unlawful. He supported his protection of mysterious discourse in Doe v. Reed (2010), composing that the Main Correction safeguards "political relationship" through marking a request.

In Tinker v. Des Moines Free People group School Locale (1969), Equity Hugo Dark dispute from the Court's perspective refuting a school's strategy to prohibit understudies from wearing armbands in dissent of the Vietnam War. Thomas embraced Dark's difference in Morse v. Frederick (2007), agreeing with restricting the reasoning of Tinker and contending that Tinker be overruled as it was an unavoidably unsupported "ocean change in understudies' discourse privileges". In his view, the Constitution doesn't prescribe whether government funded school understudies might be focused on expressive ways of behaving.

In Mahanoy Region School Area v. B.L. — in which a secondary school rebuffed an understudy for sending a profane message via online entertainment about her school, softball crew, and cheer group — Thomas was the solitary protester, favouring the school. He condemned the greater part for depending on "ambiguous contemplations" and concluded that generally schools could train understudies in comparable circumstances. He concurred with the majority's conclusion in Walker v. Texas Division, Sons of Confederate Veterans that Texas's denial of a request for a Confederate Battle Flag specialty license plate was constitutional.

7.1: Second Amendment

Thomas concurred with the judgement in McDonald v. Chicago (2010) that the option to keep and remain battle ready is material to state and nearby legislatures, however he composed a different simultaneousness observing that a singular's all in all correct to carry weapons is crucial as an honor of American citizenship under the Honors or Resistances Proviso as opposed to as a central right under the fair treatment condition. In the plurality opinion, the four justices specifically rejected incorporation under the privileges or immunities clause, "declin[ing] to disturb" the Slaughter-House Cases' ruling that the clause only applied to federal matters, as stated by the plurality.

Beginning around 2010, Thomas has disagree from refusal of certiorari in a few Second Revision cases. He casted a ballot to give certiorari in Friedman v. City of High country Park (2015), which maintained restrictions on specific quick firing rifles; In Jackson v. San Francisco (2014), ordinances similar to those struck down in Heller were upheld. Peruta v. San Diego Area (2016), which maintained prohibitive hid convey authorizing in California; furthermore, Silvester v. Becerra (2017), which maintained hanging tight periods for gun buyers who have proactively passed record verifications and as of now own guns. He was joined by Scalia in the initial two cases, and by Gorsuch in Peruta.

Thomas contradicted from the refusal of an application for a stay introduced to Boss Equity Roberts in the US Court of Allures for the Locale of Columbia Circuit case Guedes v. Department of Liquor, Tobacco, Guns, and Explosives (2019), a case testing the Trump organisation's prohibition on knock stocks. Only Gorsuch and Thomas spoke out against it.

Thomas composed the greater part assessment in New York State Rifle and Gun Affiliation, Inc. v. Bruen (2022), ensuring the right of well behaved residents to convey guns out in the open. The court ruled: At the point when the Subsequent Corrections plain text covers a singular's lead, the Constitution possibly safeguards that direct. The public authority should then legitimise its guideline by showing that it is predictable with the Country's authentic custom of gun guidelines. A court may then decide that the individual's actions fall outside the "unqualified command" of the Second Amendment. Equity Stephen Breyer, disagreeing, expressed, "when courts decipher the Subsequent Correction, it is naturally legitimate, for sure frequently vital, for them to consider the serious risks and results of weapon brutality that lead States to manage guns."

7.2: Fourth Amendment

In cases with respect to the Fourth Amendment, which disallows absurd pursuits and seizures, Thomas frequently leans toward police over litigants. For instance, his perspective for the Court in Leading body of Schooling v. Barons maintained drug testing for understudies engaged with extracurricular exercises, and he composed again for the Court in Samson v. California, allowing irregular inquiries on parolees. He contradicted in Georgia v. Randolph, which precluded warrantless hunts that one occupant supports and the other goes against, contending that the Court's choice in Coolidge v. New Hampshire controlled the case. In Indianapolis v. Edmond, Thomas depicted the Court's surviving case regulation as having held that "suspicionless road obstruction seizures are intrinsically passable whenever directed by an arrangement that restricts the watchfulness of the officials leading the stops." He expressed doubt that those cases were correctly decided, but he came to the conclusion that the Court should assume their validity and rule accordingly because the litigants in the present case had not briefed or argued that the earlier cases be overruled. In Kyllo v. United States, Thomas was in the majority, and the court ruled that the Fourth Amendment was broken when thermal imaging technology was used to search a suspect's house without a warrant.

In cases including schools, Thomas has pushed more noteworthy regard for the principle of in crazy parentis, which he characterises as "guardians delegat[ing] to educators their position to teach and keep everything under control". His dispute in Safford Brought together School Area v. Redding delineates his use of this hypothesis in the Fourth Amendment setting. School authorities in the Safford case thought that 13-year-old

Savana Redding was unlawfully circulating solution drugs. Every one of the judges agreed that it was hence sensible for the school authorities to look through Redding, and the central concern under the watchful eye of the Court was just whether the hunt went excessively far by turning into a strip search or something like that. Every one of the judges aside from Thomas presumed that the hunt disregarded the Fourth Amendment. To justify a strip search, most required evidence of danger or suspicion that drugs were concealed in a student's underwear. That's what thomas composed "sensible doubt that Redding was in control of medications disregarding these strategies, in this manner, supported a hunt stretching out to any area where little pills could be covered and that "it is a mistake for judges to assume the responsibility for deciding which school rules are important enough to allow for invasive searches and which rules are not." He added, "[t]here can be no question that a parent would have had the power to direct the hunt."

7.3: Six Amendment

In Doggett v. US, the respondent had in fact been a criminal from the time he was prosecuted in 1980 until his capture in 1988. The Court held that the postponement among prosecution and capture disregarded Doggett's 6th Amendment right to a fast preliminary, finding that the public authority had been careless in chasing after him and that he knew nothing about the prosecution. Thomas contradicted, contending that the Expedient Preliminary Statement's motivation was to forestall "'unnecessary and harsh detainment' and the 'nervousness and concern going with public allegation'" and that the case ensnared not one or the other. He cast the case rather as "present[ing] the inquiry [of] whether, free of these centre worries, the Fast Preliminary Provision safeguards a charged from two extra damages: (1) bias to his capacity to protect himself brought about by the progression of time; furthermore (2) disturbance of his life years after the supposed commission of his wrongdoing". Thomas disagreed with the court's choice to, from his perspective, answer the previous in the confirmation. He concluded that excusing the conviction "welcomes the Country's appointed authorities to enjoy impromptu and result-driven re-thinking of the public authority's investigatory endeavours. A position of this nature is not contemplated or permitted by our Constitution.

In Garza v. Idaho, Thomas and Gorsuch, in disagreement, proposed that Gideon v. Wainwright (1963), which expected that needy criminal litigants be given advice, was wrongly settled and ought to be overruled.

7.4: Eighth Amendment

Thomas was among the dissidents in Atkins v. Virginia and Roper v. Simmons, which held that the Eighth Amendment disallows the use of capital punishment to specific classes of people. In Kansas v. Swamp, his perspective for the Court demonstrated a conviction that the Constitution manages the cost of states wide procedural scope in impressive capital punishment, gave they stay inside the restrictions of Furman v. Georgia and Gregg v. Georgia, the 1976 case in which the Court switched its 1972 restriction on death penalties assuming states adhered to procedural rules.

A prisoner had been beaten in Hudson v. McMillian, resulting in a cracked lip, a broken dental plate, loose teeth, cuts, and bruises. Albeit these were not "serious wounds", the Court accepted, that's what it held "the utilisation of unreasonable actual power against a detainee might comprise savage and strange discipline despite the fact that the prisoner doesn't experience serious injury." Contradicting, Thomas expressed, "a utilisation of power that truly hurts a detainee might be corrupt, it could be tortious, it very well might be criminal, and it might try and be remediable under different arrangements of the Government Constitution, yet it isn't 'savage and uncommon discipline'. In closing, running against the norm, the Court today goes a long way past our points of reference." Thomas' vote — in one of his most memorable cases in the wake of joining the Court — was an early illustration of his readiness to be the sole protester (Scalia later joined the assessment). His viewpoint was condemned by the seven-part larger party, which said that, by contrasting actual attack with other jail conditions, for example, unfortunate jail food, it overlooked "the ideas of pride, enlightened norms, mankind, and goodness that quicken the Eighth Amendment". As per history specialist David Garrow, Thomas' difference in Hudson was a "exemplary call for government legal restriction, suggestive of perspectives that were held by Felix Sausage and John M. Harlan II an age prior, however publication analysis descended upon him". Thomas later answered the allegation "that I upheld the beating of detainees all things considered. Indeed, one must either be unskilled or loaded with malevolence to arrive at that resolution ... no legitimate pursuing can arrive at such a resolution."

Thomas co-wrote the majority opinion in United States v. Bajakajian, declaring a fine unconstitutional under the Eighth Amendment, along with the liberal justices on the Court. Failure to declare a suitcase containing more than

$300,000 on an international flight resulted in the fine. Under a government rule, 18 U.S.C. § 982(a)(1), the traveler would have needed to relinquish the whole sum. Thomas noticed that the case expected a differentiation to be made between common relinquishment and a fine demanded fully intent on rebuffing the respondent. He observed that the relinquishment for this situation was plainly planned as a discipline to some degree to a limited extent, was "terribly unbalanced" and disregarded the Exorbitant Fines Proviso.

Thomas has composed that the "Horrible and Surprising Discipline" condition "contains no proportionality standard", implying that the inquiry whether a sentence ought to be dismissed as "brutal and uncommon" relies upon the actual sentence, rather than on the thing wrongdoing is being rebuffed. He was agreeing with the Court's choice to dismiss a solicitation for survey from a candidate who had been condemned to 25 years to life in jail under California's "Three-Strikes" regulation for taking some golf clubs on the grounds that the joined

worth of the clubs made the burglary a lawful offence
and he had two past crimes in his lawbreaker record.

CHAPTER 8: Thomas More Impact Beyond The Bench

Clarence Thomas' effect reaches out a long ways past the limits of the court. His presence and choices have resounded across cultural, social, and political domains, significantly impacting different features of American life.

Leadership in Thought and Legal Philosophy:

Thomas' relentless obligation to originalism and textualism has re-imagined the talk around protected understanding. His ardent faith in complying stringently with the text of the Constitution and the law has affected legitimate researchers, molding conversations on legal limitation and the job of the legal executive in deciphering regulations.

Cultural Talk on Race and Character:

Thomas's views on race and affirmative action, as the second African American to serve on the Supreme Court, have sparked heated debate. His extraordinary point of view, frequently wandering from customary stories, has tested cultural standards and incited conversations on the intricacies of race, character, and opportunity in America.

Impact on Future Law specialists and Legitimate Personalities:

A generation of legal minds have been inspired by Thomas's jurisprudence and dissenting opinions. His opinions continue to shape the perspectives of aspiring lawyers and judges, contributing to ongoing discussions about the principles that underpin the American legal system, whether through written opinions or public speeches.

Social and Political Effect:

In addition, his presence on the Court has had an impact on politics, influencing nominations, confirmations, and the political landscape as a whole. His viewpoints on issues going from individual freedoms to the extent of government power have contributed essentially to the philosophical woven artwork of the High Court.

Enduring Influence and Legacy:

Past his nearby residency, the tradition of Clarence Thomas is ready to persevere, making a permanent imprint on legitimate ideas, the High Court's elements, and the more extensive cultural discussions around regulation, equity, and the Constitution.

Clarence Thomas' effect, subsequently, rises above the legal domain, moulding discussions and leaving an enduring engraving on the actual texture of American culture.

8.1: Race and Equivalent Insurance

Thomas accepts the Equivalent Insurance Proviso of the Fourteenth Amendment restricts thought of race, for example, race-based governmental policy regarding minorities in society or special treatment. In Adarand Constructors v. Peña, he expressed, "there is a 'moral [and] sacred identicalness' between regulations intended to enslave a race and those that disperse benefits based on race to encourage some ongoing thought of balance. Government can't make us equivalent; As equals before the law, it can only recognize, respect, and safeguard us. The fact that [affirmative action] programs may have been sparked by good intentions in part does not change the fact that the government cannot discriminate based on race under our Constitution.

In Gratz v. Bollinger, Thomas expressed, "a State's utilization of racial separation in advanced education confirmations is completely disallowed by the Equivalent Security Provision." In Guardians Engaged with Local Area Schools v. Seattle School Region No. 1, Thomas joined the assessment of Boss Equity Roberts, who concluded that "[t]he method for halting separation based on race is to quit segregating based on race." Agreeing, Thomas stated, "assuming our set of experiences has shown us anything, it has trained us to be careful with elites bearing racial hypotheses", and charged that the dispute conveyed "similitudes" to the contentions of the segregationist prosecutors in Earthy colored v. Leading body of Schooling.

In like manner, in Grutter v. Bollinger, Thomas enthusiastically cited Equity Harlan's Plessy v. Ferguson contradict: " Our Constitution is visually challenged, and neither knows nor endures classes among residents." In a simultaneousness in Missouri v. Jenkins (1995), he argued that the Missouri Locale Court "has pursued our cases to help the hypothesis that dark understudies experience the ill effects of isolation that hinders their psychological and instructive turn of events. This approach not just depends upon problematic sociology research as opposed to sacred rule, however it additionally lays on a suspicion of dark inadequacy."

A few lawful researchers have referred to Thomas' perspectives on race and the constitution as "quirky", "cynical", or "fatalistic". For instance, teachers Corey

Robin and Stephen F. Smith have portrayed Thomas' way of thinking as grounded in a type of dark patriotism that sees legislative endeavours to address prejudice as either vain or counterproductive. That view stands out from the conviction that regulations ought to be race-impartial on the grounds that racial segregation is presently not a difficult issue in the US.

Thomas joined the larger part in Understudies for Fair Confirmations v. Harvard, which struck down governmental policy regarding minorities in society in school confirmations. He recorded an agreeing assessment, which he read from the seat, an uncommon practice for High Court judges.

8.2: Abortion And Family Planning

Thomas argued that abortion is not covered by the Constitution. In Arranged Being a parent v. Casey (1992), the Court reaffirmed Roe v. Swim. Rehnquist and Scalia's dissenting opinions included Thomas and Justice Byron White. Rehnquist expressed, "[w]e accept Roe was wrongly settled, and that it can and ought to be overruled reliably with our customary way to deal with gaze decisis in sacred cases." Scalia's viewpoint inferred that the option to get a foetus removal isn't "a freedom safeguarded by the Constitution of the US". "[T]he Constitution says literally nothing regarding it," Scalia stated, "and [ ] the longstanding customs of American culture have allowed it to be lawfully abolished".

In Stenberg v. Carhart (2000), the Court struck down a state restriction on incomplete birth early termination, inferring that it bombed Casey's "unjustifiable weight" test. Thomas disagreed, expressing, "Albeit a State might allow foetus removal, nothing in the Constitution directs that a State should do as such." He proceeded to scrutinise the thinking of the Casey and Stenberg larger parts: " The greater part's emphasis on a wellbeing exemption is a fig leaf scarcely covering its aggression toward any early termination guideline by the States — an aggression that Casey suspected to dismiss."

In Gonzales v. Carhart (2007), the Court dismissed a facial test to a government restriction on halfway birth fetus removal. Agreeing, Thomas attested that the court's early termination statute had no premise in the Constitution except for that the court had precisely applied that law in dismissing the test. He added that the Court was not concluding whether or not Congress had the ability to prohibit fractional birth early terminations: "[W]hether the Demonstration comprises a reasonable activity of Congress' power under the Business Proviso isn't under the watchful eye of the Court [in this case] ... the gatherings didn't raise or brief that issue; it is outside the inquiry introduced; also, the lower courts didn't address it."

In December 2018, Thomas disagreed when the Court casted a ballot not to hear cases brought by Louisiana and Kansas to deny Medicaid subsidising to Arranged Life as a parent. Alito and Gorsuch joined Thomas' difference, contending that the Court was "abandoning its legal obligation".

In February 2019, Thomas joined three of the Court's other moderate judges in casting a ballot to dismiss a stay to briefly hinder a regulation confining fetus removal in Louisiana. The law that the court briefly remained, in a 5-4 choice, would have expected that specialists performing early terminations have conceded honours in a clinic.

In Box v. Arranged Being a parent of Indiana and Kentucky, Inc. (2019), a for each curiam choice maintaining the arrangement of Indiana's early termination limitation in regards to foetal remaining parts removal on normal premise examination and maintaining the lower court decisions striking down the arrangement prohibiting race, sex, and handicap, Thomas composed an agreeing assessment contrasting foetus removal and contraception with genetic counselling, which was drilled in the U.S. in the mid twentieth 100 years and by the Nazi government in Germany during the 1930s and 1940s, and contrasting Box with Buck v. Chime (1927), which maintained a constrained cleansing regulation in regards to individuals with mental handicaps. As he would see it, Thomas cited Margaret Sanger's help for contraception as a type of individual regenerative control that she considered better than "the revulsions of foetus removal and child murder" (Sanger's words). His viewpoint alluded a few times to antiquarian/columnist Adam Cohen's book Boneheads: The High Court, American Genetic counselling, and the Sanitization of Carrie Buck; without further ado subsequently, Cohen distributed a strongly phrased analysis saying that Thomas had confused his book and misjudged the historical backdrop of the genetic counselling development. In Box, just Thomas, Sonia Sotomayor, and Ginsburg freely enrolled their votes. In their partial and partial dissents, Ginsburg and Sotomayor stated that they would have upheld the lower court's decision to strike down the foetal remains disposal provision and the race, sex, and disability ban.

In an agreeing assessment in Dobbs v. Jackson Ladies' Wellbeing Association (2022), that's what thomas composed "any meaningful fair treatment choice is 'obviously mistaken'", and contended that the High Court ought to go past Roe versus Swim and reexamine other considerable fair treatment points of reference, incorporating those laid out in Griswold v. Connecticut (1965), Lawrence v. Texas (2003) and Obergefell v. Hodges (2015). The upsetting of these past choices would empower states to restrict admittance to contraception, condemn homosexuality, and condemn same-sex marriage, individually.

8.3: LGBTQ Rights

In Romer v. Evans (1996), Thomas joined Scalia's contradicting assessment contending that Alteration Two to the Colorado State Constitution didn't disregard the Equivalent Security Provision. The Colorado alteration disallowed any legal, regulative, or chief activity intended to safeguard people from segregation in view of "gay, lesbian, or sexually open direction, lead, practices or connections".

In Lawrence v. Texas (2003), Thomas gave a one-page contradict in which he referred to the Texas resolution disallowing homosexuality as "exceptionally senseless", an expression initially utilized by Equity Potter Stewart. He then said that assuming he were an individual from the Texas governing body he would cast a ballot to revoke the law, as it was anything but a beneficial utilization of "policing" to police private sexual way of behaving. Yet, Thomas believed that the Constitution doesn't contain a right to protection and in this way didn't cast a ballot to strike the resolution down. He considered the issue to be a matter for states to choose for themselves.

In Bostock v. Clayton District, Georgia (2020), Thomas joined Alito and Kavanaugh in contradicting the choice that Title VII of the Social equality Demonstration of 1964 safeguards representatives against segregation in view of sexual orientation or orientation. (Alito composed a difference that Thomas joined, and Kavanaugh contradicted independently.) The 6-3 decision's greater part comprised of two conservative delegated judges, Roberts and Gorsuch, alongside four

> Popularity based named judges: Ginsburg, Breyer, Sotomayor, and Kagan.

Thomas wrote a separate opinion reiterating his dissent from Obergefell v. Hodges and expressing his belief that it was wrongly decided, but he joined the other justices in denying an appeal from Kim Davis, a county clerk who refused to give marriage licenses to same-sex couples. In October 2020, Thomas wrote the opinion. In July 2021, he was one of three judges, with Gorsuch and Alito, who casted a ballot to hear an allure from a Washington flower specialist who had denied assistance to an equivalent sex couple in light of her strict convictions against same-sex marriage. In November 2021, Thomas contradicted from most of judges in a 6-3 vote to dismiss an allure from Leniency San Juan Clinical Center, a clinic partnered with the Roman Catholic Church, which had looked to deny a hysterectomy to a transsexual patient on strict grounds. Alito and Gorsuch likewise contradicted, and the vote to dismiss the allure left set up a lower court administering in the patient's approval.

8.4: Oral Contentions

During a 10-year time frame from February 2006 to February 2016, Thomas read his perspectives from the seat however posed no inquiries during oral contentions. He said in 2013 that it was "pointless in choosing cases to pose that numerous inquiries ... we ought to pay attention to attorneys who are pushing for their situations, and I figure we ought to permit the promoters to advocate." By May 2020, he had posed inquiries in two oral contentions beginning around 2006.

Thomas played a more dynamic job in addressing when the High Court moved to holding remotely coordinated contentions in May 2020 during the Coronavirus pandemic; before that, he had spoken during 32 of the approximately 2,400 contentions beginning around 1991. Since the court continued face to face oral contentions toward the start of the 2021 term, the judges consented to permit Thomas to pose the principal inquiry toward the beginning of every contention.

Thomas has given many purposes behind his quietness, including reluctance about how he talks, an inclination for paying attention to those contending the case, and trouble getting in a word. His talking and listening propensities might have been affected by his Gullah childhood, during which his English was somewhat unpolished. In a 2017 paper in Northwestern College Regulation Survey, RonNell Andersen Jones and Aaron L. Nielson concluded that while posing not many inquiries, "in numerous ways, [Thomas] is a model survey."

CHAPTER 9: Personal Life

In 1971, Thomas wedded Kathy Elegance Snare. The couple had one kid, Jamal Adeen, brought into the world in 1973, who is Thomas' only kid. Thomas and his most memorable spouse isolated in 1981 and separated in 1984.

In 1987, Thomas wedded Virginia Light, a lobbyist and helper to U.S. Agent Dick Armey. In 1997, they required Thomas' six-year-old extraordinary nephew, Imprint Martin Jr., who had lived with his mom in Savannah public lodging. Starting around 1999, Thomas and his significant other have traversed the U.S. in a motorcoach between Court terms.

Virginia "Ginni" Thomas has stayed dynamic in moderate governmental issues, filling in as an expert to The Legacy Establishment and as organizer and leader of Freedom Focal. In 2011, she ventured down from

Freedom Key to open a moderate campaigning firm, promoting her "experience and associations", meeting with recently chosen conservative delegates and considering herself an "diplomat to the Casual get-together". Likewise in 2011, 74 Majority rule individuals from the Place of Delegates composed that Equity Thomas ought to recuse himself on cases with respect to the Reasonable Consideration Act in light of "appearance of an irreconcilable situation" in view of his significant other's work.

The Washington Post detailed in February 2021 that Ginni Thomas apologised to a gathering of Thomas' previous representatives on the email listserv "Thomas Representative World" for her part in adding to a fracture connecting with "favourable to Best postings and previous Thomas assistant John Eastman, who talked at the meeting and addressed Trump in a portion of his bombed claims recorded to upset the political race results". In Walk 2022, texts between Ginni Thomas and Trump's head of staff Imprint Knolls from 2020 were gone over to the Select Board on the January 6 Assault.

The texts show Ginni Thomas more than once encouraging Glades to upset the political decision results and rehashing paranoid fears about polling form misrepresentation. Accordingly, 24 Majority rule individuals from the Place of Agents and the Senate requested that Thomas recuse himself from cases connected with endeavours to upset the consequences of the 2020 official political decision and the January 6 assault at the U.S. Legislative centre because Ginni Thomas' contribution in such endeavours brought up issues about his fair-mindedness. An April 2022 Quinnipiac survey saw that as 52% of Americans concurred that, considering Ginni Thomas' texts about toppling the aftereffects of the 2020 official political race, Thomas ought to have recused himself from related cases.

In the middle of the 1990s, Thomas was reconciled to the Catholic Church. In his self-portrait, he reprimanded the congregation for neglecting to wrestle with prejudice during the 1960s during the social liberties development, saying it was not really "unyielding about finishing bigotry then all things considered about finishing fetus removal now". Starting around 2021, Thomas is one of 14 rehearsing Catholic judges in the Court's set of experiences and one of six presently serving (alongside Alito, Kavanaugh, Roberts, Sotomayor and Barrett).

In 1975, when Thomas read financial specialist Thomas Sowell's Race and Financial matters, he tracked down a scholarly starting point for his way of thinking. The book condemns social change by the public authority and contends for individual activity to beat conditions and difficulty. Ayn Rand's works additionally impacted him, especially The Source, and he later expected his staff members to watch the 1949 film rendition of the book. Thomas recognizes "some exceptionally impressive freedom supporter leanings", however he doesn't view himself as a freedom supporter.

Thomas has said author Richard Wright is the most powerful essayist in his life; Wright's books Local Child and Dark Kid "capture[d] a ton of the sentiments that I had inside that you figure out how to subdue". Local

Child and Ralph Ellison's Undetectable Man are Thomas' two most loved books.

In 2016, Moira Smith, VP and general guidance of a flammable gas wholesaler in The Frozen North, said that Thomas grabbed her rump at an evening gathering in 1999. She helped the director of the Truman Foundation prepare for a dinner party in honor of Thomas and David Adkins as a Truman Foundation scholar. Smith's flat mates at the time affirmed that she had enlightened them regarding the occurrence. Thomas denied the claim.

Louis Blair, who was the top of the Truman Establishment and facilitated the supper at his home, said he had "no memory of the occurrence" and that he had neither seen nor known about Smith's charge. Blair recognized that he was in the kitchen more often than not thus, assuming the episode occurred, he could never have seen it, but on the other hand was "distrustful that the equity and Moira would have been separated from everyone else", considering that there were roughly 16 individuals in three rooms. Norma Stevens, who went to the occasion, said that the occurrence "could never have occurred" in light of the fact that Thomas was rarely alone, as he was the praiseworthy visitor.

In 2004, the Los Angeles Times detailed that Thomas had acknowledged gifts from Harlan Crow, a rich Dallas-based land financial backer and noticeable conservative contributor — quite a Book of scriptures, esteemed at $19,000, that once had a place with abolitionist Frederick Douglass, and a bust of Abraham Lincoln esteemed at $15,000. Crow likewise provided Thomas with a picture of the equity and his significant other, as per the painter, Sharif Tarabay. Crow's establishment gave $105,000 to Yale Graduate school, Thomas' institute of matriculation, for the "Equity Thomas Picture Asset", charge filings show.

In 2011, Politico revealed that Crow gave $500,000 to a Casual get-together gathering established by Thomas' significant other and that Thomas had neglected to report her pay on his divulgence for over 10 years. Likewise that year, the promotion bunch Normal Reason revealed that somewhere in the range of 2003 and 2007, Thomas neglected to uncover $686,589 in pay his significant other acquired from The Legacy Establishment, rather announcing "none" where "spousal non

venture pay" would be accounted for on his High Court monetary divulgence structures. The following week, Thomas said the divulgence of his significant other's pay had been "incidentally precluded because of a misconception of the documentation guidelines". He revised reports returning to 1989.

In April 2023, ProPublica announced that Thomas had "acknowledged extravagance trips practically consistently" from Crow for quite a long time and neglected to report them. They remembered trips for Crow's personal luxury plane, travels on Crow's superyacht at areas all over the planet, and stays at Crow's confidential retreat in the Adirondacks and the exclusive hangout Bohemian Woods. The Morals in Government Act requires judges, judges, individuals from Congress and administrative authorities to yearly unveil presents they get. Many chosen authorities scrutinized the presence of indecency, given Crow's gifts to moderate causes and conservative applicants, and his administration on the Leading group of Legal administrators for the American Undertaking Organization and the Hoover Establishment, which have documented amicus briefs under the steady gaze of the High Court.

Likewise in April 2023, ProPublica revealed that one of Crow's organisations purchased a house and two void parcels on a private road in Savannah, Georgia, for $133,000 in 2014. Thomas, his mother, and the surviving members of Thomas's brother's family each held equal ownership of the properties. Thomas didn't report the deal on the exposure structure he petitioned for 2014. Crow's organisation additionally paid for broad redesigns of the house, where Thomas' mom actually resides.

In May 2023, ProPublica announced that Crow had paid for non-public school educational cost for Thomas' grandnephew, Imprint Martin, of whom Thomas had legitimate care. Thomas didn't report the installments on his monetary exposure structures, while morals regulation specialists said that they were expected to be revealed as gifts. A bank explanation showed that month to month educational cost at Stowed away Lake Institute, one of the two schools Crow paid for, was $6,200. Mark Paoletta, a long-lasting companion of Thomas, said that Crow paid for one year each at Stowed away Lake and Randolph-Macon Foundation, which ProPublica assessed to add up to around $100,000.

Around the same time, The Washington Post detailed that in January 2012 moderate legal dissident Leonard Leo had conservative surveyor Kellyanne Conway's surveying firm bill the Legal Training Venture $25,000, which her firm then, at that point, paid to Ginni Thomas' firm, Freedom Counseling, for a sum of $80,000 between June 2011 and June 2012. Leo trained Conway also Thomas' name on the administrative work. The records the paper surveyed didn't demonstrate the idea of the work Thomas accomplished for the Legal Instruction Undertaking or Conway's organization. In a landmark voting rights case, the Judicial Education Project submitted a brief to the Supreme Court in 2012.

In 2023, The New York Times revealed that a companion had paid for Thomas' Prevost Le Illusion XL Long distance race RV, bought for $267,230 in 1999 (generally comparable to $469,000 in 2022). Anthony Welters, a previous UnitedHealthcare chief and a dear companion, loaned Thomas the price tag. Because of a Senate request, Welters uncovered that the credit was released in 2008, excusing a large part of the first equilibrium. A bank would have been probably not going to offer such a credit, given the Long distance race's high limit with regards to customization, which can make utilized models hard to evaluate. According to the Times, Thomas had previously stated that he "had scrimped and saved to afford the motor coach," and a friend, Armstrong Williams, stated that Thomas had stated that he "saved up all his money to buy it." At the point when the credit was pardoned, Thomas was expected to unveil the cash as a gift.

Thomas listed three flights on Crow's jets in his financial disclosure report for 2022, which he submitted in August 2023.

9.1: Praises And Acknowledgment

Thomas was granted the 1992 Horatio Alger Grant by the Horatio Alger Relationship of Recognized Americans. Thomas received the American Enterprise Institute's Francis Boyer Award in 2001. In 2012, Thomas got a privileged degree from the School of the Sacred Cross, his place of graduation. In 2020, Belmont Convent School granted him the Benedict Administration Grant for his dedication to the Catholic confidence and taxpayer supported organization.

Conclusion

In the exploration of "The Clarence Thomas Effect: Shaping The Legal History," we've traversed the remarkable journey of a jurist whose influence extends far beyond the courtroom. Clarence Thomas, an enigmatic figure in American jurisprudence, has left an indelible mark on legal history, challenging conventions, and redefining the contours of judicial discourse.

From his humble beginnings to ascending to the pinnacle of legal authority, Thomas's life story is one of resilience, conviction, and unwavering commitment to his principles. Through the pages of this book, we've uncovered the complexities of his legal philosophy, the controversies that defined his career, and the landmark decisions that have shaped the course of American law.

Thomas's impact on the Supreme Court, marked by his steadfast adherence to originalism and textualism, has not only influenced legal doctrines but also ignited debates that continue to resonate within legal circles and society at large. His perspectives on race, individual liberty, and the role of government have challenged conventional narratives, stimulating crucial conversations about the fundamental principles that underpin our legal system.

Moreover, beyond his jurisprudence, Thomas's legacy extends into the realms of culture, politics, and the aspirations of future legal minds. His dissenting opinions, impassioned speeches, and steadfast convictions have inspired a generation of thinkers and continue to shape the ideologies that define the American legal landscape.

As we conclude this exploration, the enduring legacy of Clarence Thomas remains a testament to the profound impact one individual can have on shaping legal history. His contributions, controversies, and enduring influence serve as a testament to the dynamism of the judicial process and the lasting imprint of a jurist who, through his convictions and decisions, continues to shape the very essence of American legal thought and history.

Clarence Thomas